Questions AND Answers

STARS AND PLANETS

Robin Kerrod

KINGFISHER

First published in 2000 by Kingfisher
an imprint of Macmillan Children's Books
a division of Macmillan Publishers Limited
The Macmillan Building, 4 Crinan Street, London, N1 9XW
Basingstoke and Oxford
Associated companies throughout the world
www.panmacmillan.com

ISBN 978-0-7534-0482-9

10 9 8 7 6 5 4 3 2 1
1TR/0808/(1BCA)/1200/TIMS/HBM/130MA

A CIP catalogue record is available for this book from
the British Library.

Printed in China

Illustrations: Jonathan Adams, Marion Appleton, Gary Bines
Peter Bull, Robin Carter, Chris Forsey, Lee Gibbons, Peter
Goodfellow, Jeremy Gower, Ray Grinaway, Chris Lyons,
Janos Marffy, Josephine Martin, Sebastian Quigkey,
Michael Roffe, Nick Shrewing, Guy Smith, Roger Stewart,
Ian Thompson, Rose Walton.

Contents

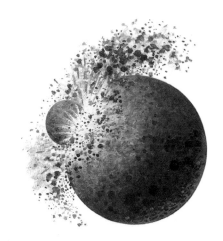

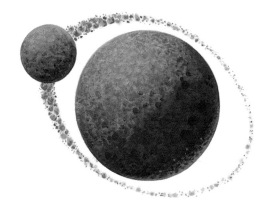

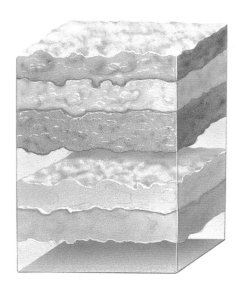

Looking at the Sky

The night sky is one of the most beautiful sights in nature. Stars beyond number shine out of a velvety blackness, bright planets wander among the stars and long-tailed comets come and go. Astronomy, the study of the night sky, is one of the most ancient sciences.

What can we see?

Although we can see a lot in the night sky with just our eyes, we can see much more through binoculars or telescopes. To the naked eye the Moon looks small, and we see few features. With binoculars and telescopes it looks larger, and we can see craters on its surface.

When did people first start studying the stars?

People must have been star-gazing for millions of years. But they probably began studying the night sky seriously only about 5,000 years ago. Early civilizations in the Middle East left records of their observations. The Babylonians were skilled observers, and we know the Egyptians were too, because they lined up their pyramids with certain constellations, or star patterns. In Britain, around 2800BCE, Stonehenge was built, possibly as a kind of observatory. Stones were lined up to show the positions of the Sun and Moon at different seasons. Ancient Chinese and Mayan astronomers left accurate records of their observations.

Stonehenge

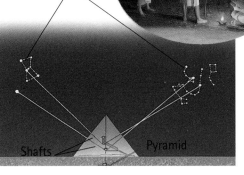

Constellations

Shafts   Pyramid

Mayan astronomer

Ancient Egyptian astronomer-priests

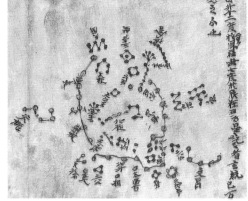

Ancient Chinese star map

Who invented telescopes?

A Dutchman named Hans Lippershey built the first telescope in 1608. But it was Galileo, an Italian, who first used one to study the night sky. He made his first observations in the winter of 1609–10. He spied the moons of Jupiter, craters on Earth's Moon and spots on the Sun. Galileo's telescope was quite small. Later devices, known as 'aerial' telescopes, were around 50 metres long.

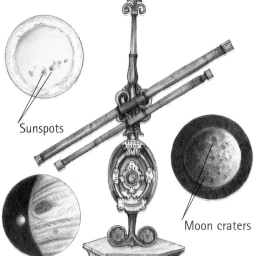

Sunspots

Jupiter   Galileo's telescope

Moon craters

Aerial telescope

How do radio telescopes work?

Stars give off radio waves as well as light waves. Astronomers have built telescopes to pick up these radio waves. Radio telescopes are not like light telescopes. Most are huge metal dishes, which can be tilted and turned to any part of the sky. The dishes pick up radio waves, or signals, and focus them onto an aerial. The signals are sent to a receiver and then to a computer, which changes them into images.

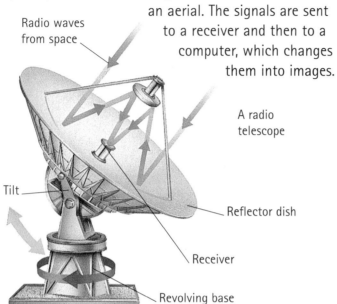

Radio waves from space

A radio telescope

Tilt

Reflector dish

Receiver

Revolving base

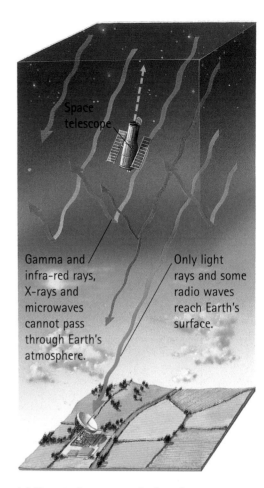

Space telescope

Gamma and infra-red rays, X-rays and microwaves cannot pass through Earth's atmosphere.

Only light rays and some radio waves reach Earth's surface.

Where do astronomers work?

Astronomers look at, or observe, the stars from observatories. The great domes on these observatories house big telescopes which use curved mirrors to collect the light from the stars. Some mirrors are as big as 10 metres across. Modern-day astronomers do not often look through these telescopes. Instead they use them as giant cameras and take pictures with them. Most observatories today are built on mountains, above the thickest part of the atmosphere, where the air is cleaner and clearer.

What is special about space telescopes?

Some of the outstanding discoveries of recent years have been made by space telescopes. Out in space, telescopes can get a much clearer view of the night sky than they can from Earth. Also, space telescopes can pick up invisible rays, such as X-rays, which cannot pass through the atmosphere.

Seeing Stars

Using just your eyes, you can see thousands of stars in the night sky. If you look closely, you will see that some are brighter than others. The bright stars make patterns that you can recognize every time you go star-gazing. We call them constellations.

The night sky in the Northern hemisphere

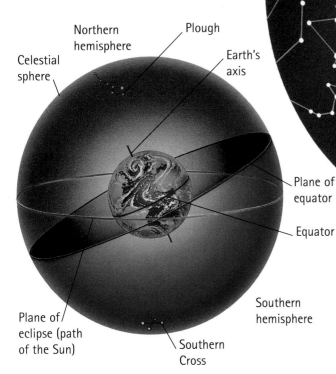

Northern hemisphere — Plough
Celestial sphere
Earth's axis
Plane of equator
Equator
Plane of eclipse (path of the Sun)
Southern hemisphere
Southern Cross

Can we all see the same stars?

Because Earth is round and just rotates on its north-south axis, we only see the stars above the hemisphere in which we live. Earth seems to be in the middle of a great dark ball, which we call the celestial sphere. People in the far north can always see the Plough but never the Southern Cross, which is seen in the far south. In the far south, no-one ever sees the Plough. People near the Equator can see almost all the stars at some time of the year.

The signs of the Zodiac

What are star signs?

During the year, the Sun appears to move through the stars of the celestial sphere. It seems to pass through 12 main constellations, called the constellations of the Zodiac. They are also called star signs, and are important in astrology. Astrologers believe that human lives are affected by the stars.

Leo the Lion   Scorpio the Scorpion

The night sky in the
Southern hemisphere

Some of the major constellations

Northern hemisphere	Southern hemisphere
1. Pegasus	1. Aquarius (The Water-bearer)
2. Perseus	2. Orion (The Hunter)
3. Pole Star	3. Scorpio (The Scorpion)
4. Plough (or Little Bear)	4. Southern Cross
5. Great Bear	5. Hydra (Water Snake)
6. Leo (The Lion)	6. Libra (Scales)

Why do the stars move across the sky?

If you go out star-gazing at night, you will notice that the constellations gradually move across the sky from east to west, as the Sun does during the day. Ancient astronomers thought that the stars were fixed on the inside of the celestial sphere, and that this sphere was spinning round Earth, which stood still. We now know that the opposite is true. It is Earth that is moving and the stars that are standing still. Earth spins round in space, moving from west to east. This makes the stars appear to travel in the opposite direction.

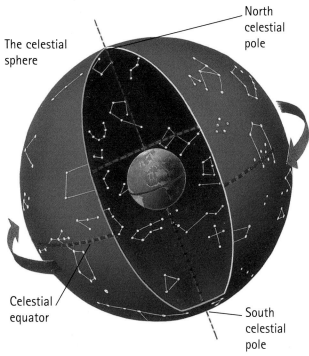

The celestial sphere

North celestial pole

Celestial equator

South celestial pole

Quick-fire Quiz

1. What's a pattern of bright stars called?
a) Congregation
b) Constellation
c) Configuration

2. From where can you see the Plough?
a) Everywhere
b) The south
c) The north

3. Which way do the stars seem to travel overhead?
a) North to south
b) East to west
c) West to east

4. How many star signs are there?
a) 10
b) 12
c) 20

Great Balls of Gas

Stars look like tiny bright specks in the night sky. But they are not tiny at all. They are in fact huge balls of searing hot gas. Stars look small only because they lie many million, million kilometres away. If you could get close to a star, you would find that it looked like our Sun, because the Sun is a star too.

Do stars last forever?

Just like living things, stars are born, grow older and, in time, die. The pictures below show two different ways in which stars die. After shining steadily for some time the stars swell up into a red giant. Some red giants shrink into a white, then a black dwarf. This will happen to the Sun one day. Other stars swell up from a red giant to a supergiant before exploding as a supernova.

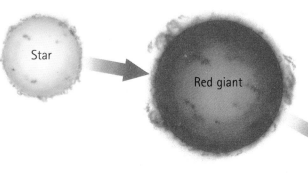

Star

Red giant

Outer layers break away

Supergiant

Quick-fire Quiz

1. What is an exploding star called?
a) Supergiant
b) Supernova
c) Superstar

2. What will our Sun be one day?
a) A supernova
b) A black dwarf
c) A black hole

3. Which is the hottest?
a) Sun
b) Red giant
c) Blue-white star

4. Which is the smallest?
a) Sun
b) Supergiant
c) Pulsar

How big are stars?

We can measure the size of one star directly because it is so close. This is our own star, the Sun. The Sun measures nearly 1,400,000 kilometres across. Astronomers can work out the size of other stars too. They have discovered that there are many stars smaller than the Sun, and also many much larger. Astronomers call the Sun a dwarf star. They know of red giant stars tens of times bigger, and supergiant stars tens of times bigger still. Some supergiants measure 400 million kilometres across.

Why do stars twinkle?

When we look up at the heavens, we can see thousands of stars shining down, but they do not give out a steady light. They seem to twinkle, or change brightness all the time. In fact they do shine steadily but air currents in the Earth's atmosphere make the starlight bend this way and that. Some of the light gets into our eyes and some is bent away. So, to us on Earth, the stars seem to twinkle.

How hot are stars?

Stars are great globes of very hot gas, but their temperature varies quite a lot. Astronomers can tell the temperature of a star by the colour and brightness of the light it gives out. Yellowish stars like the Sun have a temperature of about 5,500°C. This compares with about 3,000°C for a dim red star to 30,000°C for a bright blue-white star.

White dwarf

Dead black dwarf

Why do some stars explode?

Massive stars explode when they come to the end of their lives. They swell up into huge supergiants. Supergiants are unstable, so they collapse and blast themselves to pieces in an explosion called a supernova. Supernovae are the biggest explosions in the Universe, as bright as billions of Suns put together.

Black hole

Star

Black hole

Supernova

What makes black holes black?

After a star explodes as a supernova, what is left of it shrinks rapidly. If it is really big, it shrinks almost to nothing. All that is left is a tiny region of space that has enormous gravity. The gravity is so great that the tiny region will suck in all nearby matter, including other stars. The name 'black hole' comes from the fact that the pull it exerts is so powerful that even light cannot escape from it.

What is a pulsar?

A smaller star that explodes as a supernova ends its life as a tiny star we call a pulsar. It gets this name because it 'pulsates', or sends out pulses of energy. Astronomers think that pulsars spin round fast and send out narrow beams of energy. On Earth we see a pulse of energy when this beam sweeps past us.

A pulsar passing Earth

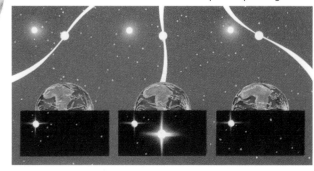

Pulsar

Galaxies

From Earth, space seems to be full of stars. But if you travelled a long way from Earth, you would in time leave the stars behind. Looking back, you would see that the stars form a kind of island in space. In other directions, you would see other star islands, which we call galaxies. The galaxies and the space they occupy make up the Universe.

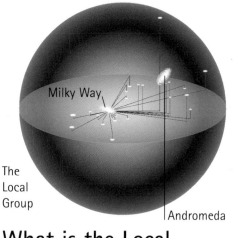

The Local Group

Milky Way

Andromeda

What is the Local Group of galaxies?

There are thousands of galaxies in space. Many are in groups called clusters. The galaxy where we live is called the Milky Way, which is in a cluster we call the Local Group. The Milky Way is the second-largest galaxy in the Local Group. The largest is the Andromeda galaxy.

Do all galaxies look the same?

Astronomers can see galaxies of all shapes and sizes through their telescopes. Some are known as barred spiral galaxies. They have curved arms coming from a bar through their centre (1). Ordinary spirals do not have the bar. Elliptical galaxies (2) have an oval shape. Galaxies with no particular shape are called irregulars (3).

How do galaxies form?

Galaxies begin to form in clouds of dark gas so huge that even light would take hundreds of thousands of years to cross them. Over time, gravity begins to pull the particles of gas together. Gradually, the gas cloud shrinks and it becomes more and more dense. Here and there it becomes dense enough for stars to form. At the same time the gas cloud starts to rotate and flatten out.

1 A huge cloud of gas shrinks and becomes denser. Stars form in the centre.

2 The starry cloud spins, and flattens into a disc shape.

3 Matter in the disc collects on arms, where more stars form.

How did the Universe begin?

Astronomers believe that the Universe began with a huge explosion known as the Big Bang. They reckon it happened more than 15,000 million years ago. The Big Bang created a hot bubble of space that has been getting bigger and bigger ever since. Astronomers believe the Universe is constantly expanding.

Big Bang

The Universe expands after the Big Bang

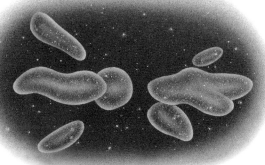

Superclusters

What makes up the Universe?

Simply speaking, the Universe is made up of matter and space. The matter is found as planets, moons and stars. The stars gather together into great galaxies, and the galaxies gather into groups, or clusters. Even the clusters gather together to form gigantic superclusters of galaxies. The Universe is made up of millions of these superclusters.

The Milky Way – a spiral galaxy

What are quasars?

Quasars look like stars. But they are so far away that, for us to detect them, they must be brighter than thousands of galaxies together. Astronomers think quasars get their great power from black holes. As matter is sucked into a black hole, enormous energy is given out as light and other radiation.

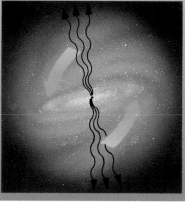

Quick-fire Quiz

1. What is the galaxy our Sun and its planets are in called?
a) The Heavens
b) The Milky Bar
c) The Milky Way

2. Which of these is brightest?
a) Star
b) Quasar
c) Galaxy

3. What began the Universe?
a) Gravity
b) Black holes
c) The Big Bang

4. Which of these is the Universe doing?
a) Expanding
b) Exploding
c) Shrinking

The Solar System

Every day, the Sun appears to travel across the Earth's sky from east to west. In fact Earth circles the Sun. Earth is part of the Sun's family, or Solar System. It is one of eight bodies called main planets that circle the Sun. Pluto used to be counted as a planet, but now it is known as a dwarf planet.

How big is the Solar System?

Earth is nearly 150 million kilometres from the Sun. This seems a huge distance, but it is only a small step in space. The furthest planets lie thousands of millions of kilometres away from the Sun. The diagram on the right shows the orbits, or paths, of the eight main planets and the dwarf planet Pluto around the Sun.

Who first realized that Earth travels round the Sun?

Early astronomers thought the Sun and other planets circled the Earth. Nicolaus Copernicus (1473–1543) was a Polish priest and astronomer. He came up with the theory that the Sun was the centre of the Universe, and that Earth and the planets moved round it. This was the first real challenge to the idea that Earth was the centre of the Universe, which ancient astronomers believed. Copernicus published his theory while he lay dying in 1543, but religious leaders opposed his ideas for many years.

What happened at the birth of the Solar System?

1 The Solar System was born in a great cloud of gas and dust about 5,000 million years ago. There are many clouds like this, called nebulae, in the space between the stars.

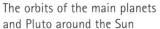
The orbits of the main planets and Pluto around the Sun

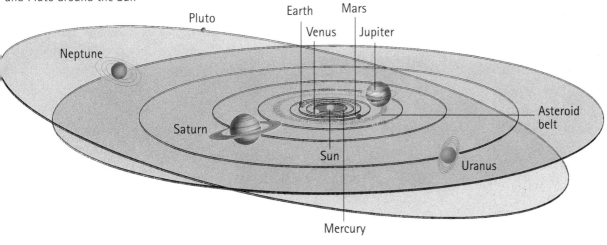

Pluto
Neptune
Earth
Mars
Venus
Jupiter
Saturn
Sun
Asteroid belt
Uranus
Mercury

Quick-fire Quiz

1. What is a nebula?
a) A kind of star
b) A kind of cloud
c) A kind of planet

2. How far away from Earth is the Sun?
a) 1.5 million km
b) 15 million km
c) 150 million km

3. How many main planets are in orbit around the Sun?
a) Ten
b) Nine
c) Eight

4. How many years old is the Solar System?
a) 50 million
b) 500 million
c) 5,000 million

2 Some parts of the cloud became much denser. Gas and dust in these areas started to stick together under the pull of their gravity. In time they formed into a ball-shaped mass.

3 The ball shrank and warmed up. Slowly, it started to glow, forming a 'baby' Sun by the time it was about 100,000 years old.

4 The baby Sun was spinning rapidly, flinging off masses of material into space. All the while it was shrinking and getting hotter and hotter.

5 In time, the baby Sun became hot enough to set off nuclear reactions. These produced the fantastic energy it needed to shine as a 'grown-up' star.

6 The ring of material thrown out earlier by the Sun began to clump together. It gradually formed larger and larger lumps at different distances from the Sun.

7 The large lumps grew into the planets we find today. Smaller lumps formed the moons of the planets, and even smaller lumps formed the asteroids.

13

Our Star, the Sun

The Sun is our local star. Like the other stars, it is a ball of very hot gas. It lies about 150 million kilometres from Earth, and is about 1.4 million kilometres across. The Sun pours huge amounts of energy into space. The light and heat that reach Earth make life possible.

Hydrogen atoms

Helium atom

Energy

Where does the Sun get its energy?

The energy that keeps the Sun shining is produced in its centre, or core. The pressure in the core is enormous, and the temperature reaches 15 million °C. Under these conditions, atoms of hydrogen gas fuse (join together) to form another gas, helium. This process is called nuclear fusion. It produces enormous amounts of energy.

What is the Sun's surface like?

The Sun's surface is a bubbling, boiling mass of very hot gas, constantly in motion, like a stormy sea. Here and there, fountains of flaming gas thousands of kilometres high shoot out. These are called prominences. Eventually, they curve over and fall back. Violent explosions called flares also often take place, blasting particles into space that can cause magnetic storms on Earth.

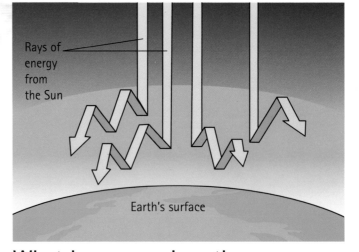

Rays of energy from the Sun

Earth's surface

What happens when the Sun warms Earth?

The Sun pours energy on to Earth, warming the land and the water in the oceans. Gases in the air trap the heat and warm the atmosphere. They act like a greenhouse, so the warming process is called the 'greenhouse effect'. One of the main gases that traps heat is carbon dioxide, produced when fuels burn.

Quick-fire Quiz

1. What is an explosion on the Sun called?
a) Prominence
b) Flare
c) Sunspot

2. What produces the Sun's energy?
a) Burning coal
b) Burning hydrogen
c) Nuclear fusion

3. Which gas in air traps heat?
a) Nitrogen
b) Carbon dioxide
c) Oxygen

4. How many more years will the Sun last?
a) 50 million
b) 500 million
c) 5,000 million

Is it safe to look at the Sun?

Never look directly at the Sun. Its light is so bright that it will damage your eyes and can even blind you. Instead, use binoculars or a telescope to throw an image onto paper, and look at that.

What is the Sun like inside?

The Sun is made up of a number of layers. In the centre is the very hot core, where energy is produced. This energy travels outwards by radiation, reaching the outer layer, called the convection region. There, currents of hot gas carry the energy to the surface (photosphere), where it escapes as light and heat. The temperature of the surface is about 5,500°C. Sunspots are dark patches on the surface. They are about 1,000°C cooler. Some sunspots grow to be bigger than Earth.

How do eclipses happen?

Occasionally, the Moon moves across the face of the Sun during the day, blotting out its light and casting a dark shadow on Earth. Day turns suddenly into night. We call this a total eclipse of the Sun. Eclipses occur because, from Earth, the Moon seems to be almost the same size as the Sun and can cover it up. Total eclipses can only be seen over a small part of Earth because the Moon casts only a small shadow.

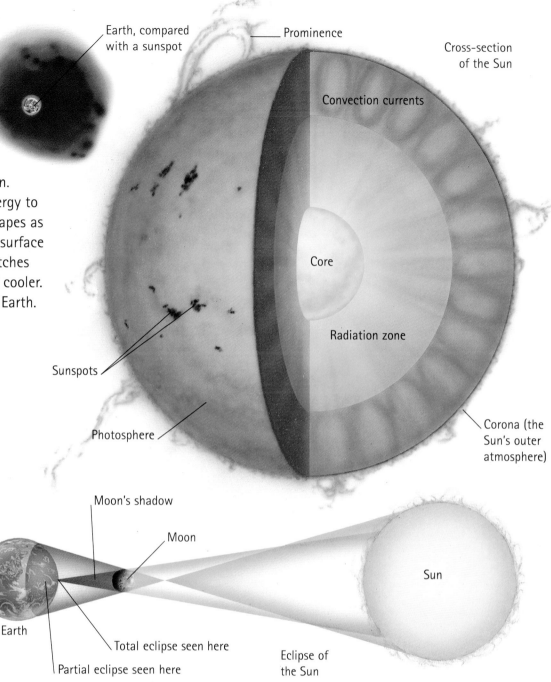

Earth, compared with a sunspot

Prominence

Cross-section of the Sun

Convection currents

Core

Radiation zone

Sunspots

Photosphere

Corona (the Sun's outer atmosphere)

Moon's shadow

Moon

Sun

Earth

Total eclipse seen here

Partial eclipse seen here

Eclipse of the Sun

Will the Sun always shine?

1 The Sun was born, along with the rest of the Solar System, about 5,000 million years ago. It has been shining steadily ever since.

2 In another 5,000 million years' time, the Sun will swell up and get hotter. Earth's oceans will boil away and all life will die.

3 As the Sun gets bigger and hotter and redder, Earth will be scorched to a cinder. In time it may be swallowed by the Sun's outer layers.

4 Gradually, the red giant Sun will begin to shrink again. Eventually it will become a white dwarf star about the size of Earth.

The Planets

The eight main planets are the most important members of the Sun's family. In order of distance from the Sun, they are Mercury, Venus, Earth, Mars, Jupiter, Saturn, Uranus and Neptune. The first four are small rocky bodies. The next four are giants, made up mainly of gas.

Jupiter

Sun

Mercury

Venus

Earth

Mars

How big are the planets?

The pictures on these two pages show the relative sizes of the planets. You might think that Earth is a big place. But look how much bigger some of the other planets are! Even the biggest planets, however, are dwarfed by the Sun. The Sun is nearly ten times bigger across than Jupiter, and it could swallow more than a million Earths. However, Earth is bigger than three of the main planets – nearby Venus, Mars and Mercury.

Which is the biggest planet?

Jupiter is by far the largest of the planets. It has more mass than all the other planets put together. It measures nearly 143,000 kilometres across, which is 11 times bigger than Earth. Even though it is so big, it takes less than 10 hours for it to spin round once. This means that its surface is spinning round at a speed of 45,000 kilometres an hour. This is 30 times faster than Earth spins.

Which planets have rings?

Once it was thought that Saturn was the only planet that had rings around it because they were the only ones that can be seen through a telescope. But close-up photographs taken by the *Voyager* space probes have shown us that the other three gas giants – Jupiter, Uranus and Neptune – have rings too. The rings around these other planets are much thinner, narrower and darker than Saturn's.

Why is Uranus sometimes called 'new'?

Astronomers have been studying the planets for thousands of years. They have watched the way they move, or 'wander', across the night sky, unlike the stars. But the ancient astronomers could only see five planets in the night sky. It was not until 1781 that someone built a telescope powerful enough to spot another planet, which came to be called Uranus. Uranus was the first 'new' planet to be discovered. Neptune was discovered in 1846. Pluto was discovered in 1930, and it was known as the ninth planet until 2006.

Uranus

What is special about Saturn?

Two things are outstanding about Saturn. One is obvious when you look at the planet through a telescope. The planet is surrounded by a set of bright, shining rings. Many people think that these make Saturn the most beautiful object in the Solar System. The other special thing about Saturn is that it is the lightest (least dense) of all the planets. It is lighter even than water. This means that if you could place it in a huge bowl of water, it would float.

Rings

Saturn

Quick-fire Quiz

1. Which of these has rings?
a) Earth
b) Saturn
c) Venus

2. How many planets are bigger than Earth?
a) Two
b) Three
c) Four

3. How fast does Jupiter spin?
a) 4,500 km/h
b) 45,000 km/h
c) 450,000 km/h

4. When was the last main planet discovered?
a) 1781
b) 1846
c) 1979

Which planet is furthest from the Sun?

The most distant of the main planets is Neptune, at 4,500 million kilometres from the Sun. The dwarf planet Pluto is usually further away than this, but sometimes it travels inside Neptune's orbit, making it nearer to the Sun than Neptune for long periods at a time. This was the case for 20 years between 1979 and 1999. You can see a diagram of these planets' orbits on page 13.

Pluto

Neptune

17

Mercury

Mercury is the planet closest to the Sun. It is also the fastest-moving planet, whizzing round the Sun in just 88 days. Being close to the Sun, Mercury gets extremely hot. Its surface is covered in thousands of craters, making it look rather like the Moon.

Mercury

Earth

How big is Mercury?

Mercury is the smallest of the main planets. With a diameter of only 4,880 kilometres, it is less than half the size of the Earth.

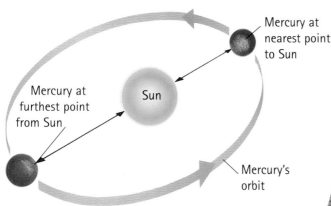

Mercury at nearest point to Sun

Mercury at furthest point from Sun

Sun

Mercury's orbit

What is strange about Mercury's orbit?

Most planets have a nearly circular orbit, or path, around the Sun. Mercury, however, has an oval orbit. At times it travels as far as 70 million kilometres away from the Sun. At others, it gets as close as 46 million kilometres.

Why does Mercury get so hot?

As it travels around the Sun, Mercury spins so slowly on its axis that a point on its surface stays in the Sun for nearly six Earth-months at a time. With the Sun so close and shining for so long, surface temperatures on Mercury soar to 430°C – hot enough to melt metals such as tin and lead.

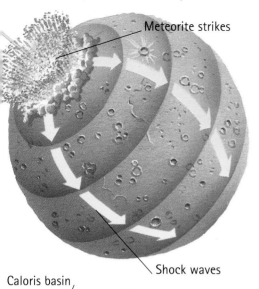

Meteorite strikes

Shock waves

Caloris basin

Craters

What has shaped Mercury's surface?

Billions of years ago, all the planets were bombarded by huge meteorites. On Earth, most craters made by the meteorites have been worn away by the action of the weather. Mercury has no weather because it has almost no atmosphere. So all the craters that formed ages ago remain, and the whole planet is covered with them. A huge one, called the Caloris Basin, was made by a giant meteorite that sent shock waves throughout the planet.

What is Mercury made of?

Like the Earth and the other rocky planets, Mercury is made up of different layers. Underneath a rocky crust there is a rocky mantle, and, at the centre, a huge metal core. The shrinking of the core has caused great ridges, up to 3 kilometres high, to appear on the surface.

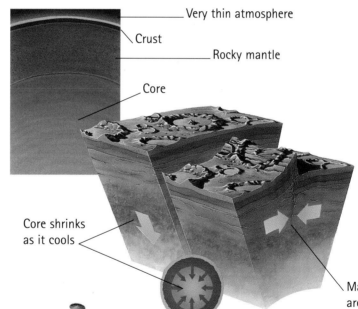

Very thin atmosphere

Crust

Rocky mantle

Core

Core shrinks
as it cools

Mantle and crust
are squeezed

Have any space probes visited Mercury?

Only one space probe has flown to study Mercury. Named *Mariner 10*, it flew to the planet in 1974, after visiting Venus. Its pictures revealed for the first time that Mercury looked rather like some parts of the Moon. *Mariner 10* flew past Mercury twice more. On the last occasion, in March 1975, it skimmed only about 300 kilometres above the surface.

Mariner 10

MERCURY DATA

Diameter at equator: *4,880km*
Mass: *0.06 times Earth's mass*
Average distance from Sun:
58 million km
Minimum distance from Earth:
91 million km
Length of day: *59 Earth-days*
Length of year: *88 Earth-days*
Temperature: *-185°C to 430°C*
Satellites: *0*

Venus

Venus is the planet whose orbit comes closest to Earth. We often see it shining in the western sky after sunset, which is why it is known as the Evening Star. Venus is a near twin of Earth in size, but it is a waterless world with a scorching climate.

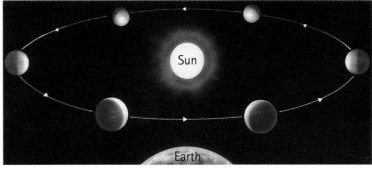

Venus in orbit

Why does Venus change shape?

From Earth, Venus seems to change its shape and size as time goes by. This is because it orbits closer to the Sun than Earth. When it is on the far side of the Sun, we see it as a small circle. As it moves closer to Earth, it gets bigger, but we only see it as a part-circle. Finally, it is just a thin crescent.

What is the surface of Venus like?

Space probes have shown that great plains cover much of Venus' surface. There are two big highland regions, which we can think of as continents. One is found in the north, and is called Ishtar Terra. The other lies near the equator, and is called Aphrodite Terra.

Venus landscape

Clouds cover the surface of Venus

Why is Venus so cloudy?

We cannot see Venus' surface from Earth because of thick clouds in its atmosphere. These clouds are not like the clouds we find on Earth, which are made up of tiny water droplets. Venus' clouds are made up of tiny droplets of sulphuric acid, one of the strongest acids we know. The sulphur has found its way into the atmosphere from the many volcanoes that have erupted on Venus over the years.

How can we see through Venus' clouds?

Space probes can see through Venus' clouds and show us what the planet's surface is like. But they do not 'see' in ordinary light. They 'see' with radar beams, because radar beams can go straight through clouds. The most successful radar probe, named *Magellan*, mapped the whole planet between 1990 and 1992.

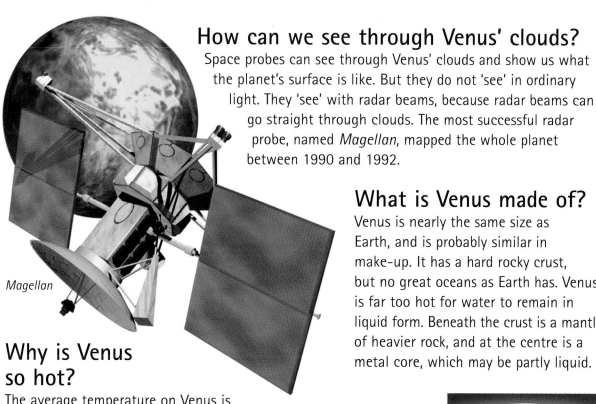

Magellan

What is Venus made of?

Venus is nearly the same size as Earth, and is probably similar in make-up. It has a hard rocky crust, but no great oceans as Earth has. Venus is far too hot for water to remain in liquid form. Beneath the crust is a mantle of heavier rock, and at the centre is a metal core, which may be partly liquid.

Why is Venus so hot?

The average temperature on Venus is more than twice as hot as an oven set on 'high'. This is because its atmosphere contains mainly carbon dioxide – a heavy gas that traps heat. Over the years it has caused the atmosphere to trap more and more heat, as a greenhouse does. The cloud layers trap the heat too, making the temperature reach a scorching 480°C.

Venus' atmosphere

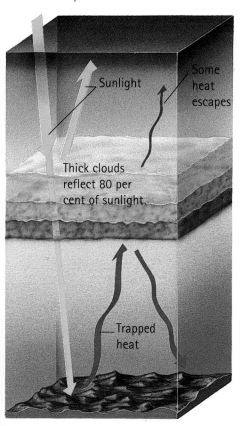

Sunlight

Some heat escapes

Thick clouds reflect 80 per cent of sunlight

Trapped heat

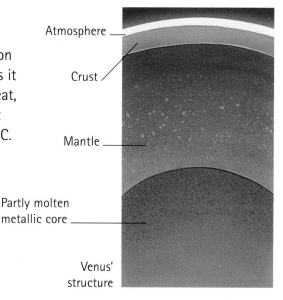

Atmosphere

Crust

Mantle

Partly molten metallic core

Venus' structure

VENUS DATA

Diameter at equator: 12,100km
Average distance from Sun: 108 million km
Minimum distance from Earth: 42 million km
Turns on axis: 243 Earth-days
Circles Sun: 225 Earth-days
Surface temperature: 480°C
Satellites: 0

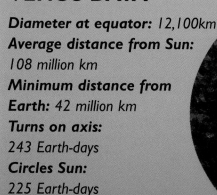

Earth

From space our home planet, Earth, appears to be mainly blue in colour. This is because of the colour of the oceans which cover over two-thirds of its surface. The land areas, or continents, cover less than a third. The layer of air above the surface is thin, but makes life on Earth possible.

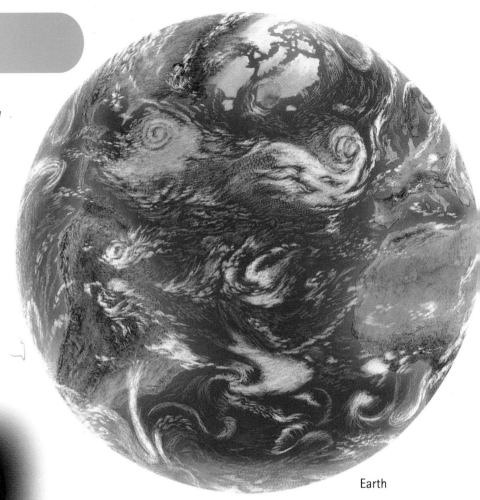

Earth

What causes day and night?

Almost every place on Earth has a time when it is light (day), followed by a time when it is dark (night). Day and night come about because Earth spins round in space, and different parts of its surface face the Sun. It is daytime when a place is on the side of Earth facing the Sun. It becomes night when the place is on the side of Earth facing away from the Sun.

What makes Earth different?

A number of things make Earth different from the other planets. It is covered with great oceans of water, and its atmosphere contains lots of oxygen. The atmosphere also acts like a blanket, holding in enough of the Sun's heat to keep Earth at a comfortable temperature. The water, the oxygen and the temperature make Earth a suitable place for living things – at least one-and-a-half million different kinds of plants and animals.

Earth land and seascape

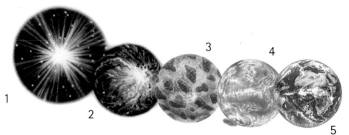

1

2

3

4

5

How has Earth changed?

Earth formed about 4,600 million years ago when bits of matter in space came together (1). At first Earth was a great molten ball (2). It gradually cooled and the atmosphere and oceans eventually formed (3). In time, it changed into the world we know today (4 and 5), made up of layers of rock with a metal core. Our world is still changing. Currents in the rocks beneath the crust are widening the oceans, and driving the continents further apart (see below).

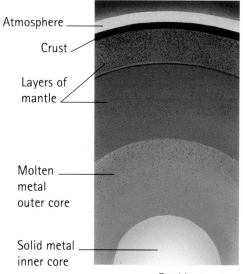

Atmosphere

Crust

Layers of mantle

Molten metal outer core

Solid metal inner core

Earth's structure

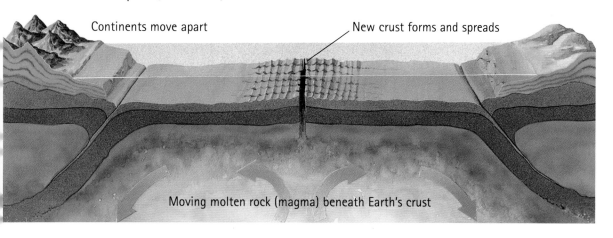

Continents move apart

New crust forms and spreads

Moving molten rock (magma) beneath Earth's crust

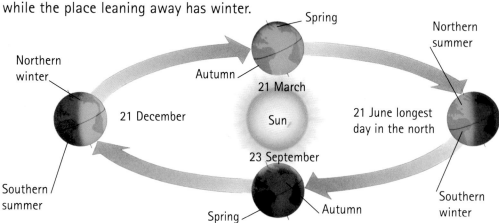

Over thousands of years, Earth's orbit changes from circular to elongated.

EARTH DATA

Diameter at equator: 12,756km
Average distance from Sun: 149.6 million km
Turns on axis: 23 hours 56 minutes
Year length: 365.25 days
Surface temperature: -89°C to 58°C
Satellites: I (the Moon)

What causes the seasons?

The changes in weather that we call the seasons happen because of the way Earth's axis is tilted in space. Because of this tilt, a place leans more towards the Sun and is warmer at some times of the year than at others. It is this that causes the changing seasons. The place tilted towards the Sun has summer, while the place leaning away has winter.

Spring

Northern summer

Northern winter

Autumn

21 March

Northern summer

21 December

Sun

21 June longest day in the north

23 September

Southern summer

Spring

Autumn

Southern winter

23

The Moon

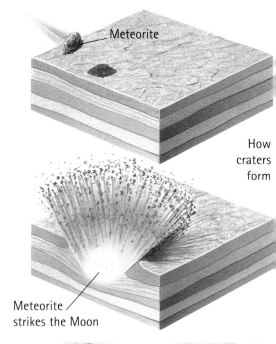

Meteorite

How craters form

Any object, or satellite, which orbits a planet is called a moon. Our Moon circles Earth once a month and is Earth's nearest neighbour in space. We can see it clearly through telescopes, and astronauts have explored it on foot. It is a small body – about a quarter the diameter of Earth. It has no atmosphere, no weather and no life.

Meteorite strikes the Moon

How did the Moon form?

Most astronomers think that the Moon formed after another large body smashed into Earth thousand of millions of years ago (1). Material from Earth and the other body were flung into space. In time, this material came together to form the Moon (2). This explains why Moon rocks are different from rocks on Earth.

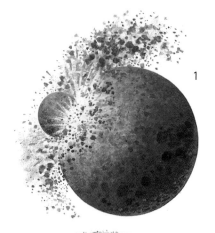

1

2

Terraced crater

Concentric crater

Ray crater

Ghost crater

When did astronauts land on the Moon?

The first astronauts landed on the Moon on July 20, 1969. They were Edwin Aldrin and Neil Armstrong, the crew of the lunar landing module of the *Apollo 11* spacecraft. Armstrong was the first person to stand on the Moon. There were five more lunar landings – one more in 1969, two in 1971, and two in 1972.

Moon rock

What made the Moon's craters?

The surface of the Moon is covered with many thousands of pits, or craters. They have been made by meteorites raining down from outer space. Most large craters have stepped, or terraced, walls and mountain peaks in the middle. The largest craters are more than 200 kilometres across. Some young craters have bright streaks, or rays, coming from them, while only the tips of some old 'ghost' craters can be seen.

Where are the Moon's seas?

Early astronomers thought that the dark areas we see on the Moon might be seas. They called them 'maria', the Latin word for 'seas'. We know now that they are vast dusty plains, but we still call them seas. Most seas are found on the side of the Moon that always faces us, the near side. There are only one or two small seas on the opposite side, the far side.

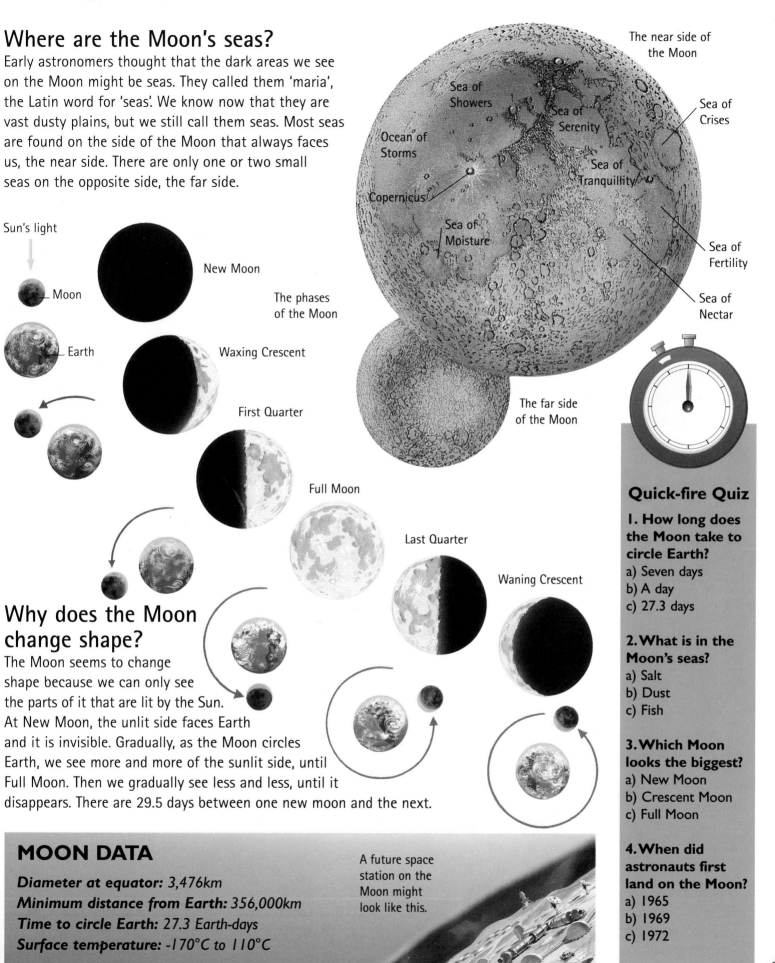

The near side of the Moon

Sea of Showers

Ocean of Storms

Sea of Serenity

Sea of Crises

Sea of Tranquillity

Copernicus

Sea of Moisture

Sea of Fertility

Sea of Nectar

The far side of the Moon

Sun's light

Moon

New Moon

Earth

The phases of the Moon

Waxing Crescent

First Quarter

Full Moon

Last Quarter

Waning Crescent

Why does the Moon change shape?

The Moon seems to change shape because we can only see the parts of it that are lit by the Sun. At New Moon, the unlit side faces Earth and it is invisible. Gradually, as the Moon circles Earth, we see more and more of the sunlit side, until Full Moon. Then we gradually see less and less, until it disappears. There are 29.5 days between one new moon and the next.

MOON DATA

Diameter at equator: 3,476km
Minimum distance from Earth: 356,000km
Time to circle Earth: 27.3 Earth-days
Surface temperature: -170°C to 110°C

A future space station on the Moon might look like this.

Quick-fire Quiz

1. How long does the Moon take to circle Earth?
a) Seven days
b) A day
c) 27.3 days

2. What is in the Moon's seas?
a) Salt
b) Dust
c) Fish

3. Which Moon looks the biggest?
a) New Moon
b) Crescent Moon
c) Full Moon

4. When did astronauts first land on the Moon?
a) 1965
b) 1969
c) 1972

Mars

Small and red in colour, Mars is more like Earth than any other planet. People once believed that intelligent beings lived on Mars – but space probes have shown that there are no Martians, and no other life on the planet. It is too cold, and the atmosphere is too thin for life to exist.

Mars' atmosphere

Thick cloud

Carbon dioxide gas

Dust-clouds

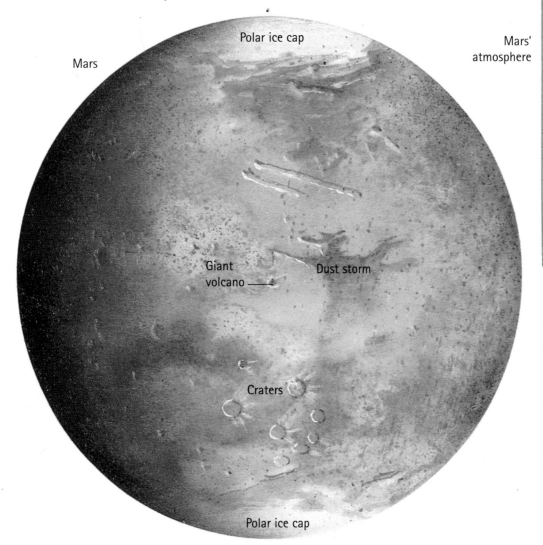

Mars

Polar ice cap

Giant volcano

Dust storm

Craters

Polar ice cap

Why is Mars called the 'Red Planet'?

Astronomers call Mars the 'Red Planet' because of its colour. Its surface is reddish-orange. This colour comes from the rust-like iron minerals in the surface rocks and soil.

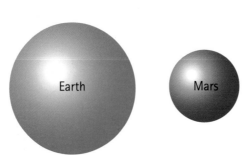

Earth

Mars

How is Mars made up?

Mars is a rocky planet and it has a similar make-up to Earth. It has a hard crust, a rocky mantle and an iron core. Its atmosphere, however, is very much thinner than Earth's. The atmospheric pressure on Mars is only about a hundredth of what it is on Earth. The main gas in the Martian atmosphere is carbon dioxide, instead of nitrogen and oxygen, as on Earth. There is very little moisture in the atmosphere, and no oceans, lakes or rivers. Around the cold poles, the moisture freezes to form the planet's ice caps. Although Mars is similar to Earth in some ways, it is a lot smaller.

MARS DATA

Diameter at equator: 6,787km
Average distance from Sun:
228 million km
Minimum distance from Earth:
56 million km
Turns on axis:
24 hours 37 minutes
Circles Sun: 687 Earth-days
Surface temperature:
-110°C to 0°C
Satellites: 2

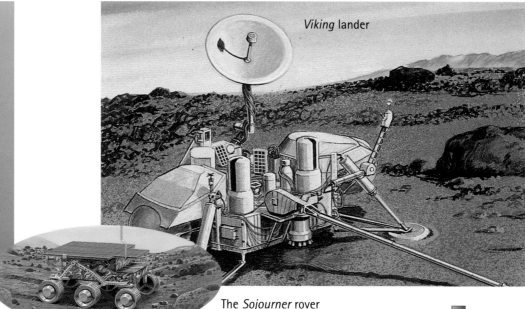

Viking lander

Deimos

Phobos

The Sojourner rover

Does Mars have moons?

Mars has two small moons, Phobos and Deimos. Phobos is the larger, but it is less than 30 kilometres across. Astronomers believe they were once asteroids, captured by Mars' gravity.

Which space probes explored Mars?

In 1965, *Mariner 4* flew past Mars and sent back pictures. *Mariner 9* went into orbit round it in 1971. Five years later two *Viking* craft dropped landers onto the surface. In 1997, the *Pathfinder* probe landed, carrying a small vehicle called *Sojourner*, which investigated the surrounding rocks. More rovers were sent to Mars in 2003, and still more are planned.

Quick-fire Quiz

1. What colour is Mars?
a) Yellow
b) Blue
c) Red

2. What is Mars' atmosphere made up of?
a) Oxygen
b) Carbon dioxide
c) Sulphur dioxide

3. What was the name of the Mars rover?
a) *Sojourner*
b) *Surveyor*
c) *Mariner*

4. What were Mars' moons originally?
a) Planets
b) Comets
c) Asteroids

Dust storm

Olympus Mons and the surface of Mars

Mars' structure

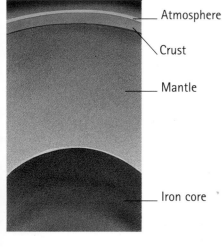

Atmosphere

Crust

Mantle

Iron core

What is Mars' surface like?

Mars' surface is dotted with vast deserts, craters and volcanoes. The highest volcano, Olympus Mons, is nearly 30 kilometres high. There is also a gash in the surface over 4,000 kilometres long and 7 kilometres deep in places. It has been called Mars' Grand Canyon, but its proper name is Mariner Valley. Smaller valleys look as if they have been made by flowing water, so astronomers think that Mars may once have had rivers and seas.

Jupiter

Jupiter is the giant among the planets. All the others could fit into it with room to spare, and it could swallow more than 1,300 bodies the size of Earth. Jupiter is a gassy planet, made up mainly of hydrogen. Its stormy atmosphere is full of clouds. Jupiter travels through space with a large family of moons, some as big as planets.

What makes Jupiter so colourful?

The coloured 'stripes' we see on Jupiter are different kinds of clouds in the thick atmosphere. Because Jupiter spins round quickly, these clouds are drawn out into bands parallel with the equator. The paler bands are called zones and the darker ones are called belts.

Jupiter's ring

What is Jupiter made of?

Jupiter is a great ball of gas and liquid gas. Its atmosphere is more than 1,000 kilometres deep and is made up mainly of hydrogen gas, with some helium. It is full of clouds of ice, ammonia and ammonium compounds. At the bottom of the atmosphere the great pressure turns the hydrogen into a liquid. Deeper down, rapidly increasing pressure turns the hydrogen into a kind of liquid metal. Right at the centre, there is a small core of rock.

The Great Red Spot

Jupiter's atmosphere

Tops of clouds

Hydrogen gas

Crystals of ammonia ice

Ammonium sulphide

Droplets of water ice

Liquid hydrogen

Jupiter's structure

Atmosphere

Liquid hydrogen

Liquid metallic hydrogen

Rocky core

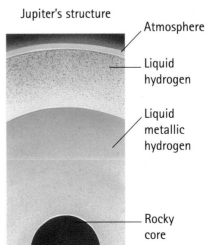

The Great Red Spot

Europa

Callisto

Io

Ganymede

Surface of Io

Erupting volcano

What's special about Io?

Io has been nicknamed the 'pizza moon' because it is so colourful. It is a very unusual moon because it has active volcanoes on it. These pour out liquid sulphur, which is a rich yellow-orange, giving Io its brilliant and varied colours. The *Voyager 1* probe discovered Io's volcanoes when it flew past Jupiter in 1979.

How many moons does Jupiter have?

Jupiter has at least 63 moons. We can see the four biggest with binoculars. The Italian astronomer Galileo discovered them in 1610, so they are known as the Galilean moons. In order of distance from Jupiter, they are Io, Europa, Ganymede and Callisto. With a diameter of 5,262 kilometres, Ganymede is the largest of Jupiter's moons and, at roughly the same size as planet Mercury, is the biggest moon in the Solar System.

JUPITER DATA

Diameter at equator: 142,800km
Average distance from Sun:
778 million km
Minimum distance from Earth:
590 million km
Turns on axis: 9 hours 50 minutes
Circles Sun: 11.9 Earth-years
Temperature at cloud tops: -150°C
Satellites: 63 known

What is the Great Red Spot?

The most prominent feature on Jupiter's surface is a large red oval region called the Great Red Spot. Astronomers did not know what it was until space probes looked at it closely. We now know it is a gigantic swirling storm, rather like a huge hurricane on Earth. It measures about 40,000 kilometres across – three times the size of Earth.

Which probes have visited Jupiter?

Pioneer 10 flew past Jupiter in 1973 and took the first close-up photographs of its colourful atmosphere. *Pioneer 11* followed the next year, and travelled on to Saturn. *Voyagers 1* and *2* flew past in 1979, sending back astounding pictures and information. In 1995, the *Galileo* probe went into orbit round Jupiter after dropping a probe into its atmosphere.

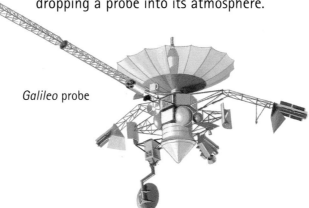

Galileo probe

Saturn

Saturn is the second biggest planet, after Jupiter. Like Jupiter, it is a giant ball of gas. Saturn is a favourite planet among astronomers because of its shining rings. The rings appear to change shape year by year as the planet makes its way round the Sun.

SATURN DATA

Diameter at equator: 120,000km
Diameter of visible rings: 270,000km
Average distance from Sun:
   1,427 million km
Minimum distance from Earth:
   1,200 million km
Turns on axis: 10 hours 40 minutes
Circles Sun: 29.5 Earth-years
Temperature at cloud tops:
   -170°C
Satellites: at least 57

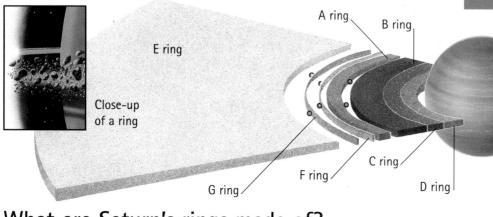

E ring

Close-up of a ring

A ring

B ring

C ring

F ring

G ring

D ring

What are Saturn's rings made of?

Saturn is surrounded by many rings, but only three can be seen from Earth – the A, B and C rings. The other rings were discovered by space probes. The rings look like solid sheets, but they are not. They are made up of millions upon millions of bits of ice, whizzing round the planet at high speed. The bits vary in size from specks of dust to large chunks. In places, the rings are less than 50 metres thick.

Saturn's atmosphere

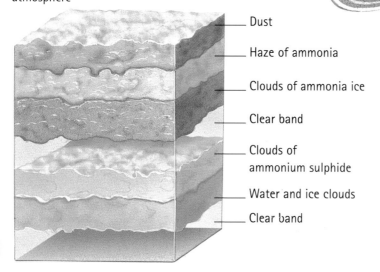

Dust

Haze of ammonia

Clouds of ammonia ice

Clear band

Clouds of ammonium sulphide

Water and ice clouds

Clear band

Why is Saturn so cloudy?

Saturn is a very cloudy planet. The clouds form into bands parallel to the equator because the planet is spinning round so fast. These bands are not as easy to see as they are on Jupiter because of the haze that tops the atmosphere. There seem to be three main cloud layers on Saturn, located at different levels, with clear areas in between. The upper layers of clouds are made up of ammonia and ammonium compounds. At the lowest level, the clouds seem to be made up of water and ice particles, like the clouds we have on Earth.

What's Saturn like inside?

Saturn is a gas giant, which means that it is composed mainly of gas and liquid gas. Its cloudy atmosphere is made up almost entirely of hydrogen and helium. Below that lies a vast, deep ocean of liquid hydrogen. Deeper down is a layer of hydrogen in the form of a liquid metal. At the centre of the planet, there is a small core of rock.

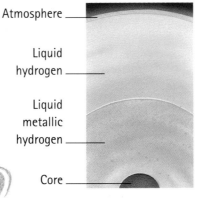

Atmosphere ___

Liquid hydrogen ___

Liquid metallic hydrogen ___

Core ___

Saturn's structure

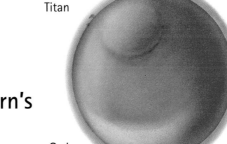

Titan

What are Saturn's moons like?

Saturn has at least 57 moons. Only five have a diameter greater than 1,000 kilometres – Tethys, Dione, Rhea, Titan and Iapetus. The smallest, Pan, is only about 20 kilometres across. Biggest by far is Titan. With a diameter of 5,140 kilometres, it is the second largest moon in the whole Solar System, and the only one that has a thick atmosphere.

Saturn

What is Titan's surface like?

Titan's thick atmosphere is made up mainly of nitrogen gas. It is orange in colour and full of hazy clouds that stop us seeing what its surface is like. In 2005, the *Cassini* space probe dropped a landing probe (*Huygens*) on the surface of Titan, to find out information about the conditions there. Data gathered by the probe showed evidence of huge lakes or seas of liquid methane or ethane.

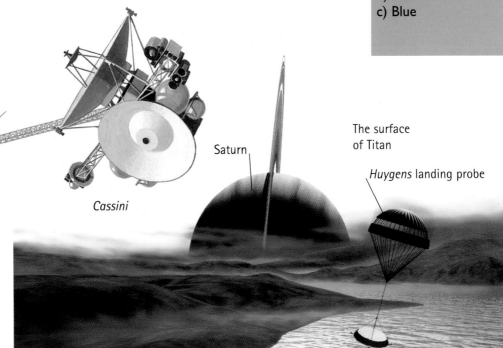

Cassini

Saturn

The surface of Titan

Huygens landing probe

Uranus

Uranus is the third biggest planet, and is four times bigger across than Earth. It is so far from the Earth that it is barely visible with the naked eye. Because of this it was not discovered until the 1700s, with the help of a telescope.

Why is Uranus sometimes called the topsy-turvy planet?

All planets spin as they orbit the Sun. We say they spin round their axis (an imaginary line that goes through their north and south poles). In most planets the axis is nearly upright as the planet spins. But Uranus spins on an axis at right-angles to normal, so it is as if Uranus is lying on its side. This means that, at times in its orbit, Uranus' poles point straight at the Sun. As a result, they become hotter than the rest of the planet, instead of always being colder, as on Earth.

Who discovered Uranus?

In March 1781, an English astronomer named William Herschel was looking at the sky through a telescope. He spied what he thought must be a new comet, but it was actually a new planet. Until then, astronomers knew of only six planets. The new planet, which was later called Uranus, turned out to be twice as far away from the Sun as Saturn.

How many rings does Uranus have?

Astronomers used to think that Saturn was the only planet that had rings circling it. But, in 1977, they discovered that Uranus had rings too. There are about 11 main rings, made up of bits of rock up to a metre across, which whizz round the planet at high speed. The particles in some of the rings are kept in place by tiny 'shepherd' moons.

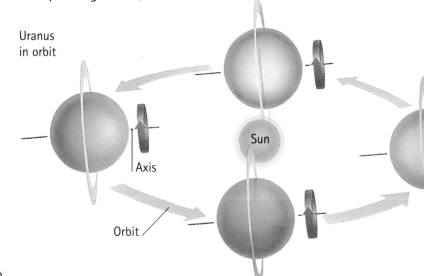

Uranus in orbit

Sun

Axis

Orbit

Direction of Uranus' rotation

Which probe has visited Uranus?

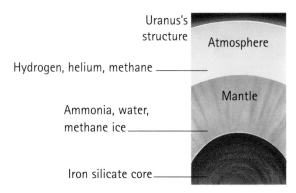

Voyager 2

We can find out very little about Uranus through telescopes because it is so far away. Most of what we know comes from the *Voyager 2* space probe, which visited Uranus in 1986. *Voyager 2* had earlier visited Jupiter (1979) and Saturn (1981). It flew past Neptune in 1989 and is now far beyond all the planets, journeying further into space.

Uranus's structure

Hydrogen, helium, methane

Atmosphere

Mantle

Ammonia, water, methane ice

Iron silicate core

What is Uranus made of?

Uranus has a thick atmosphere of hydrogen, helium and methane, and a mantle of water, ammonia and methane ice. At the centre there is an iron silicate core.

What are Uranus' moons like?

We can only see the five largest of Uranus' moons from Earth – Miranda, Ariel, Umbriel, Titania and Oberon. Ten smaller moons were discovered by *Voyager 2*. The large moons are great balls of rock and ice, pitted with craters, and with long cracks in their surface. Titania is the biggest moon. It is about 1,600 kilometres across.

Miranda

Ariel

Titania

URANUS DATA

Diameter at equator:
51,000km
Average distance from Sun:
2,870 million km
Minimum distance from Earth: 2,600 million km
Turns on axis:
17 hours 14 minutes
Circles Sun: 84 Earth-years
Temperature at cloud tops:
-200°C
Satellites: 27 known

What is special about Miranda?

Miranda is the smallest moon that can be seen from Earth, with a diameter of only about 500 kilometres. Close-up photographs show it to be the most interesting moon of all. Its surface is a patchwork of different kinds of landscape - craters, grooves, cliffs and valleys. Astronomers think that, ages ago, Miranda shattered into pieces when it collided with another body. Then the pieces came together to create the landscape we see today.

The surface of Miranda

Quick-fire Quiz

1. What makes Uranus unique?
a) It has many moons
b) Its large size
c) A highly tilted axis

2. What do shepherd moons keep in place?
a) Space sheep
b) Meteorites
c) Ring particles

3. When was Uranus discovered?
a) In 1681
b) In 1781
c) In 1881

4. Which is Uranus' biggest moon?
a) Miranda
b) Ariel
c) Titania

Neptune and Pluto

Neptune and the dwarf planet Pluto lie thousands of millions of kilometres away from Earth, at the edge of the Solar System. Neptune, a main planet, is a gas giant, very like Uranus. Pluto is a tiny ice ball, smaller than our own Moon.

Why is Neptune blue?

Neptune is a lovely blue colour, rather like Earth. This colour comes about because the atmosphere contains a gas called methane. Methane absorbs the red colours in sunlight, and makes the light coming from Neptune's atmosphere appear blue. Dark spots that sometimes appear in Neptune's atmosphere are violent storms.

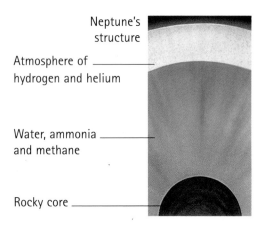

Neptune's structure

Atmosphere of hydrogen and helium

Water, ammonia and methane

Rocky core

Does Neptune have moons?

Through a telescope, we can see two moons circling around Neptune – Triton and Nereid. When *Voyager 2* visited the planet, it found six more. One, Proteus, was slightly bigger than Nereid, but the others were tiny. More have been found since. As the picture shows, Triton is by far the biggest moon, measuring some 2,700 kilometres across. Unusually, it circles the planet in the opposite direction from most moons.

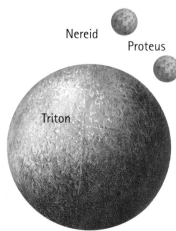

Nereid

Proteus

Triton

What is Neptune like?

Neptune has a similar make-up to its twin planet, Uranus. It has an atmosphere made up mainly of hydrogen, together with some helium. Beneath this there is a huge, deep, hot ocean of water and liquid gases, including methane. In the centre, there is a core of rock, which may be about the same size as Earth.

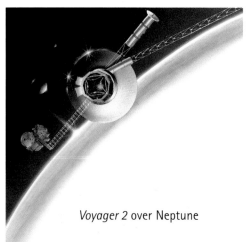

Voyager 2 over Neptune

When did Voyager 2 visit Neptune?

Neptune was the last planet *Voyager 2* visited on its 12-year journey. Launched in 1977, *Voyager 2* passed about 5,000 kilometres above Neptune's cloud tops on August 24, 1989 – closer than to any other planet. By then, it was more than 4,000 million kilometres from Earth, and its radio signals took more than four hours to get back.

NEPTUNE DATA

Diameter at equator:
49,500km
Average distance from Sun:
4,500 million km
Minimum distance from Earth:
4,300 million km
Turns on axis: 17 hours 6 minutes
Circles Sun: 165 Earth-years
Temperature at cloud tops:
-210°C
Satellites: 13 known

PLUTO DATA

Diameter at equator: 2,250km
Average distance from Sun:
5,900 million km
Minimum distance from Earth:
4,300 million km
Turns on axis: 6 Earth-days 9 hours
Circles Sun: 248 Earth-years
Surface temperature: -230°C

Who found Pluto?

Percival
Lowell

United States astronomer
Percival Lowell built his
own observatory, and led
a search for a ninth
planet. An astronomer
who worked there, Clyde
Tombaugh, finally
discovered it in 1930.

Charon

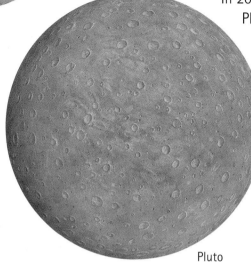

Pluto

Is Pluto a planet?

When Pluto was discovered, it was counted as
a planet – number nine in the Solar System. Since then,
astronomers have found out more about it and realized it
is different from the eight main planets, and they have
found other objects a bit like Pluto.
In 2006, they reclassified
Pluto as a dwarf planet.

What do we know about Pluto?

We do not know much about Pluto because it is
so far away. At its furthest, it travels more than
7,000 million kilometres from the Sun. Even with
powerful telescopes, it looks only like a faint star.
All we know is that Pluto is a deep-frozen ball
of rock and ice. It probably has a covering of
'snow', made up of frozen methane gas. Near
it is Charon, which may be a moon of Pluto
or it may be another dwarf planet.

Pluto's structure

Thin atmosphere of
methane and nitrogen

Mantle of ice

Rocky core

What would Charon look like from Pluto?

Charon circles Pluto in the same time it takes Pluto to spin round
once. This makes Charon appear fixed in Pluto's sky, and it can only
be seen from one side of the planet. From that side,
Charon would appear huge, much bigger than
the Moon does on Earth. This is because
Charon circles very close to
Pluto, only about 20,000
kilometres away.

Quick-fire Quiz

1. Which is
largest?
a) Charon
b) Neptune
c) Pluto

2. Which is
Neptune's
biggest moon?
a) Charon
b) Nereid
c) Triton

3. Who discovered
Pluto?
a) Percival Lowell
b) Clyde Tombaugh
c) William Herschel

4. Voyager 2
reached Neptune
from Earth after
how long?
a) 5 years
b) 9 years
c) 12 years

Charon seen from Pluto

Asteroids and Meteoroids

There are many bodies in the Solar System besides the planets and their moons. They are mostly lumps of rock or ice. The biggest ones, called asteroids, can be hundreds of kilometres across. The smallest, called meteoroids, can be as tiny as grains of sand.

How big are asteroids?

Ceres, the biggest asteroid, is about 1,000 kilometres across. It was discovered in 1801. Pallas and Vesta are about 550 kilometres across. Most asteroids are just a few tens of kilometres across.

Ceres

A meteor

What is a fireball?

Most of the meteoroids that enter Earth's atmosphere are tiny specks. But some are as big as pebbles. These larger meteoroids burn for longer and more brightly, and create the flaming objects we call fireballs.

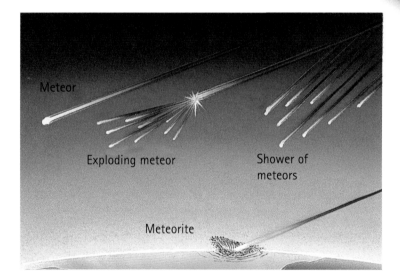

Meteor

Exploding meteor

Shower of meteors

Meteorite

What is the difference between a meteor and a meteorite?

Meteoroids are invisible unless they collide with the Earth's atmosphere, when they become streaks of light, known as meteors or 'shooting stars'. When a group of meteoroids all burn together, we see a meteor shower. Meteorites are simply meteors that have fallen to Earth. Some are made of rock, others mainly of the metals iron and nickel.

Aurorae (Northern and Southern lights)

Spacecraft

Meteors

How high up do meteors occur?

Meteoroids from outer space shower down on Earth all the time. When they are about 120 kilometres above the ground, the air rubs against them and makes them glow white hot. When this happens, we see the streaks of light we call meteors.

Where do you find asteroids?

Most asteroids are found in a broad ring about midway between the orbits of Mars and Jupiter. Astronomers call the ring the asteroid belt. But some asteroids travel outside the belt. A few occasionally come dangerously close to Earth. Two small groups of asteroids, the Trojans, circle the Sun in Jupiter's orbit. The picture below shows the orbits of some of the more unusual asteroids.

Where did the asteroids come from?

Until quite recently, astronomers believed that the asteroids were the remains of another planet. They believed that this planet came too close to Jupiter and was pulled apart by Jupiter's gravity. But astronomers today think that the asteroids are a collection of lumps that never gathered together to form a planet or a moon.

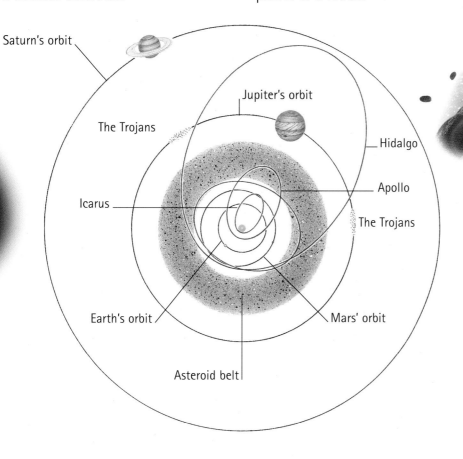

Saturn's orbit

Jupiter's orbit

The Trojans

Hidalgo

Icarus

Apollo

The Trojans

Earth's orbit

Mars' orbit

Asteroid belt

Did a meteor kill the dinosaurs?

When meteorites or asteroids fall to Earth, they create pits, or craters. Big meteorites can create enormous craters, like the famous Meteor Crater in Arizona, United States. This measures more than· 1,200 metres across and is about 180 metres deep. A huge crater near the Mexican coast was formed 65 million years ago by a falling asteroid. Many scientists think the impact changed Earth's climate, killing the dinosaurs and many other species.

Arizona Meteor Crater

Quick-fire Quiz

1. What is a shooting star?
a) An exploding star
b) An asteroid
c) A meteor

2. Which of these hit the ground?
a) Fireballs
b) Meteorites
c) Meteors

3. Which is the biggest asteroid?
a) Vesta
b) Arizona
c) Ceres

4. What do asteroids circle round?
a) The Sun
b) Jupiter
c) Saturn

Comets

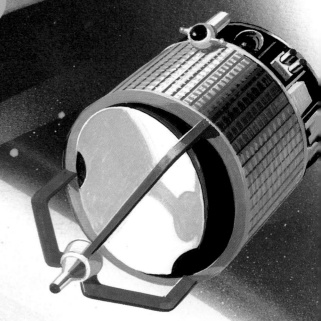

Comets are small members of the Solar System. They are lumps of ice and dust. Most of the time, they are found in the outermost parts of the Solar System, where we cannot see them. They only become visible when they travel in towards the Sun and start to melt. Then they may become bright enough to shine like beacons in the sky.

Which probes have visited comets?

Giotto was one of five space probes sent to meet Halley's comet in 1986. Launched by the European Space Agency, it sent back close-up pictures of the comet's head and nucleus. The others were Russia's *Vega 1* and *Vega 2* and Japan's *Sakigake* and *Suisei*. In 2004, the *Stardust* spacecraft collected particles from the coma of Comet Wild 2, and in 2005, the *Deep Impact* probe blasted a crater on Comet Tempel 1.

Edmond Halley

Which is the most famous comet?

Halley's comet is probably the most famous of all the comets. It was named after the English astronomer Edmond Halley (1656–1742). He saw a comet in 1682, and reckoned that it was the same one that had been seen in 1531 and 1607. He suggested that it turned up about every 76 years, and would do so again in 1758. It did exactly as he had predicted and, since then, it has been called Halley's comet. Ancient records show that Halley's comet has been seen regularly since 240BCE. It appeared last in 1986, and it will return next in 2061. In 1986, it was only just visible to the naked eye. Two more recent comets, Hyakutake in 1996 and Hale-Bopp in 1997, were very much brighter.

Why do comets have tails?

When a comet is a long way from the Sun we cannot see it, and it is frozen solid. As it travels in towards the Sun, it warms up. Some of its icy surface melts and turns to gas. This mixes with escaping dust to form a cloud. The cloud shines in the sunlight, and the comet becomes visible. As the comet gets nearer the Sun, the gas and dust cloud gets bigger. The sunlight exerts a kind of pressure that forces the gas and dust away from the comet's head, forming a tail. After the comet has looped round the Sun, it begins to cool. Its shining head and tail shrink and fade away.

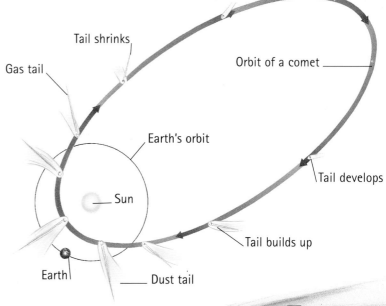

Tail shrinks

Gas tail

Orbit of a comet

Earth's orbit

Sun

Tail develops

Tail builds up

Earth

Dust tail

How big is the comet's nucleus?

As it travels across the sky, a comet may stretch for hundreds of thousands of kilometres. That is the size of the billowing cloud of gas and dust that forms the comet's head and tail. The solid part of the comet, its nucleus, is very much smaller and only a few kilometres across.

Crumbling particles of rock and ice

Jets of gas given off

Nucleus

Can comets hit the planets?

On its way in towards the Sun, a comet may travel close to one of the planets. When this happens, the comet is pulled from its normal path by the planet's gravity. If the comet gets too close, it will end up hitting the planet. In 1994, pieces of a broken-up comet named Shoemaker Levy 9 smashed into the planet Jupiter. Each time a piece hit the atmosphere, it created a great fireball, which blasted out great clouds of gas.

Quick-fire Quiz

1. What makes comets have tails?
a) Gravity
b) Sunlight
c) Starlight

2. When was Halley's comet first recorded?
a) 2000BCE
b) 240BCE
c) 1066CE

3. A comet has recently hit which planet?
a) Jupiter
b) Neptune
c) Mars

4. Which is the smallest part of a comet?
a) Head
b) Tail
c) Nucleus

Index

Quick-fire Quiz ANSWERS

Page 5 Looking at the Sky
1. b   2. c   3. b   4. b

Page 7 Seeing Stars
1. b   2. c   3. b   4. b

Page 8 Great Balls of Gas
1. b   2. b   3. c   4. c

Page 11 Galaxies
1. c   2. b   3. c   4. a

Page 13 The Solar System
1. b   2. c   3. c   4. c

Page 14 Our Star the Sun
1. b   2. c   3. b   4. c

Page 17 The Planets
1. b   2. c   3. b   4. b

Page 19 Mercury
1. b   2. c   3. b   4. a

Page 21 Venus
1. c   2. b   3. c   4. a

Page 23 Earth
1. b   2. b   3. c   4. a

Page 25 The Moon
1. c   2. b   3. c   4. b

Page 27 Mars
1. c   2. b   3. a   4. c

Page 29 Jupiter
1. c   2. a   3. c   4. b

Page 31 Saturn
1. c   2. b   3. b   4. a

Page 33 Uranus
1. c   2. c   3. b   4. c

Page 35 Neptune and Pluto
1. b   2. c   3. b   4. c

Page 37 Asteroids
1. c   2. b   3. c   4. a

Page 39 Comets
1. b   2. b   3. a   4. c